Level
2

The Nature Kid's Guide to
PRAIRIE DOGS

DAVID ANDERSON

LP Media Inc. Publishing
Text copyright © 2026 by LP Media Inc.
All rights reserved.

For information address LP Media Inc. Publishing,
30012 Variolite St NW, Princeton MN 55371
www.lpmedia.org

Publication Data

Prairie Dogs
The Nature Kid's Guide to Prairie Dogs — First edition.

Summary: "Learn all about Prairie Dogs, the Nature Kid Way"
— Provided by publisher.

ISBN: 979-8-89818-169-7

[1. Prairie Dogs – Non-Fiction] I. Title.

Title: The Nature Kid's Guide to Prairie Dogs

CONTENTS

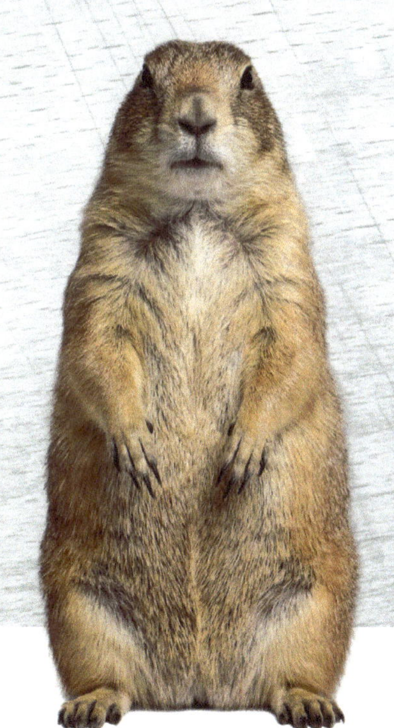

PRAIRIE PARADISE

Prairie dog towns once covered 100 million acres. One Texas **colony** had 400 million prairie dogs! It stretched for hundreds of miles.

Chirp chirp! A prairie dog stands tall. It watches over the plains.

Prairie dogs live in flat grasslands. They need wide spaces. They need short grass. Tall plants block their view. They cannot see danger. These animals stay away from forests. They stay away from mountains too.

The ground must be just right for them to live there. Prairie dogs dig deep tunnels. They need dry, hard soil. If the soil is wet or too sandy it falls apart.

Grasslands get hot in summer. They also get freezing in winter. Prairie dogs handle both well. Their underground homes stay cool in heat and warm when snow falls.

DOG MAP

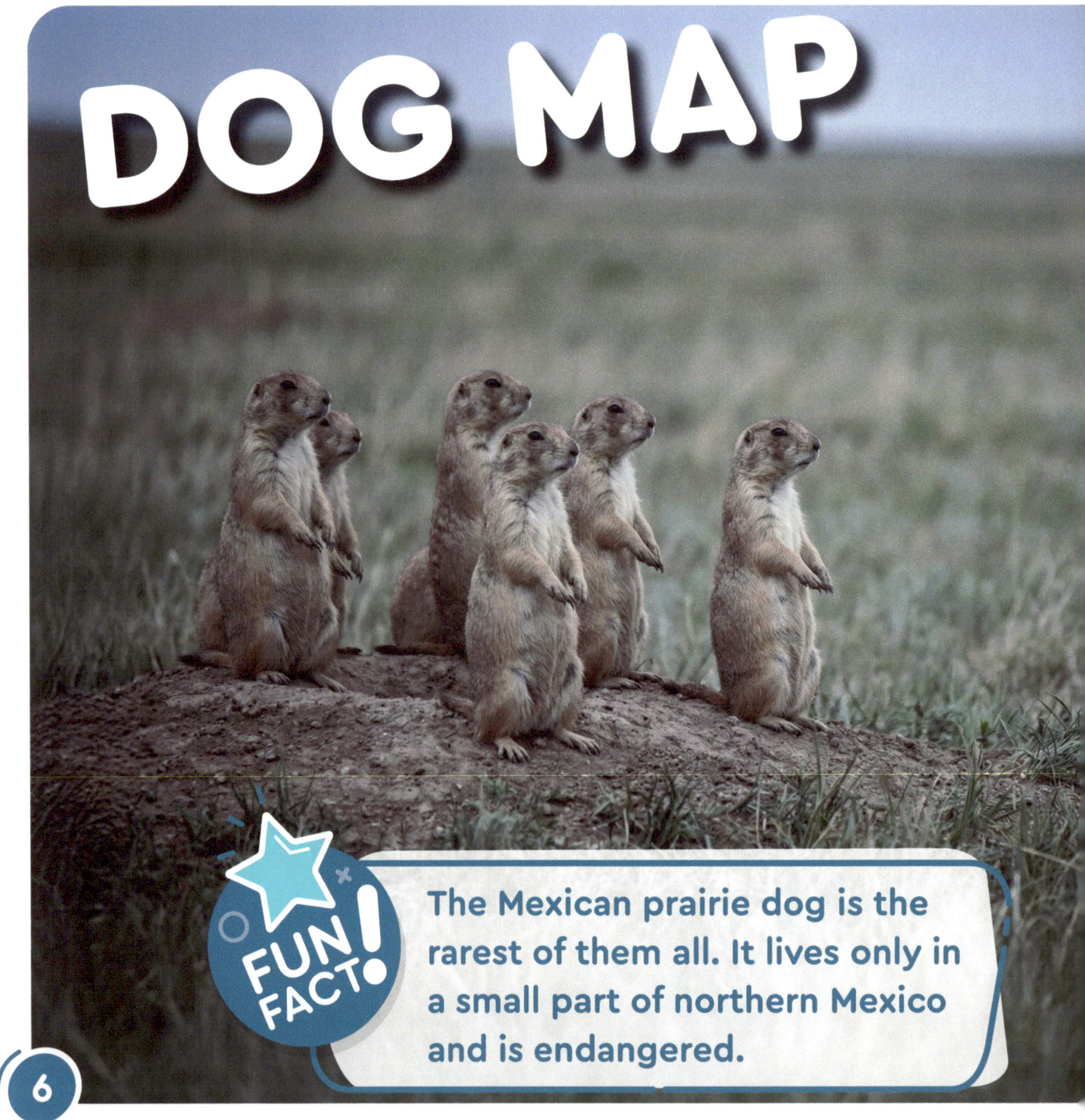

The Mexican prairie dog is the rarest of them all. It lives only in a small part of northern Mexico and is endangered.

Look! A prairie dog family looks out from their burrow. They always check for safety before leaving.

Prairie dogs live only in North America. You won't find them anywhere else! They live from Canada to Mexico.

Black-tailed prairie dogs live in the central United States. White-tailed prairie dogs live further west. They live in Wyoming and Colorado.

Gunnison's prairie dogs live in the Four Corners region. Utah prairie dogs live only in Utah.

Even though they live in different places, all prairie dogs share a love for digging, chattering, and living together in big family groups.

PINT SIZED

Chirp! A tiny prairie dog pops up. It looks around from its burrow.

Prairie dogs are small animals. A full-grown prairie dog is 12 to 17 inches long. They look about the size of a fat squirrel (with no tail).

These animals weigh only 1 to 3 pounds. Males are usually a little bigger than females.

A prairie dog can stand on its back legs. It stands about 12 inches tall. This helps it fit in its tunnels. Standing tall is also how they do their famous warning bark!

Prairie dogs in the north are bigger than in the south. The extra body size helps them stay warm during long, freezing winters.

BUILT TO BURROW

Scratch A prairie dog digs deep into the earth. Its claws scrape dirt.

Prairie dogs have bodies made for digging. Their front paws have long, curved claws. These sharp claws loosen the hard soil. Then their paws kick dirt out of the tunnel.

Their teeth are special too. Prairie dogs have four big front teeth that never stop growing! Chewing roots and dirt wears them down.

Prairie dogs also have small, round ears. Their small ears keep dirt out. Their eyes sit high on their heads. This helps them spot danger while peeking out of **burrows**.

SUPER
SENSES

Screech! The prairie dog spots danger far away. Its eyes scan the sky.

Prairie dogs have excellent eyesight. Their eyes can see almost all around them. They spot hawks flying high in the sky.

Their hearing is very sharp too. Prairie dogs hear sounds that humans cannot.

Prairie dogs also use smell to stay safe. They sniff the air for danger. Their noses also help them find food.

Prairie dogs can see blue and yellow, but they cannot see the color red!

DUSTY DISGUISE

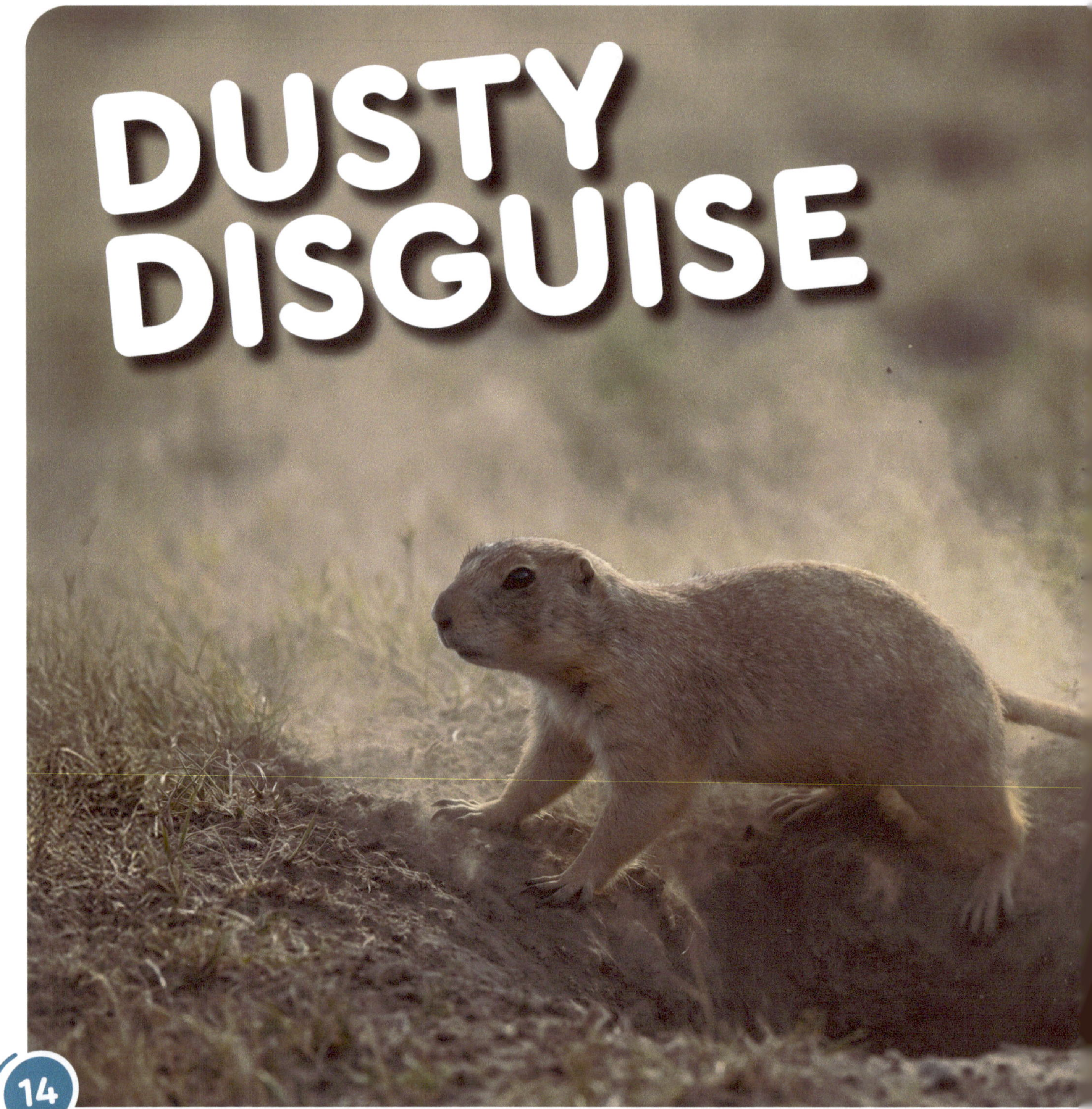

Crouch! A prairie dog dives toward his burrow, his brown fur blends in with the dirt and dust.

Prairie dogs have tan and brown fur. This color matches the dry grass around them. This makes it hard for **predators** to spot them from far away.

Their fur changes with the seasons. In summer, they have thin fur. In winter, they grow a thick, warm coat.

Prairie dogs also stay very still when danger is near. They freeze in place to hide.

Prairie dogs flatten against the ground to hide from hawks and eagles above.

GRASS GRAZERS

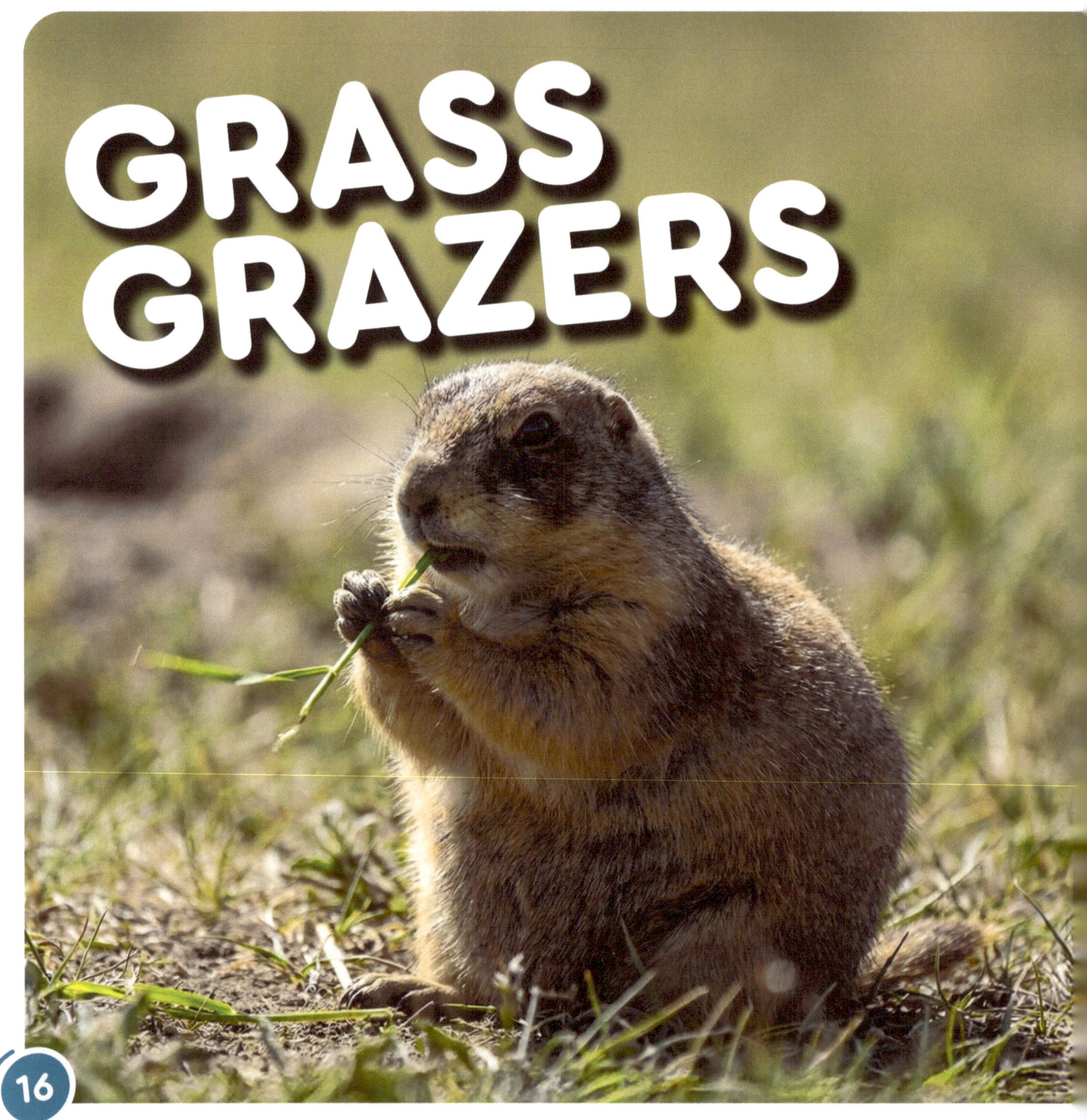

Chomp! Tiny teeth tear through grass. A prairie dog enjoys its meal.

Grass makes up about 60 to 90 percent of a prairie dog's diet. They munch on stems, leaves, and seeds all year long.

They also eat other plants like roots and flower buds. In spring, they nibble on fresh green shoots.

Prairie dogs sometimes eat insects too. Grasshoppers are one of their favorites. They also snack on beetles and caterpillars when they find them.

Prairie dogs get all their water from plants. They never need to drink!

BARK BACK

FUN
FACT!

Prairie dogs can describe what a predator looks like using just their barks, including its size and color!

Bark! The prairie dog sees danger. It calls out loud.

Prairie dogs are great talkers. They make many sounds. Each sound means something.

They bark to warn of danger. One fast bark means a hawk is diving. Many barks in a row mean a coyote is near.

These animals are friendly too. They touch noses to say hello. They groom each other. This shows they are friends. Scientists think that when they jump-yip means 'all clear.' It may also check if neighbors are watching.

DANGER
ABOVE

Screech! A hawk circles above. A shadow flies over the burrow.

Many animals hunt prairie dogs.

Hawks swoop down from the sky. Eagles dive down too. Golden eagles can dive at 200 miles per hour!

Coyotes chase prairie dogs on the ground. Badgers dig into their burrows. Black-footed ferrets live in the tunnels. They hunt at night.

Rattlesnakes hunt young prairie dogs. With so many hunters, prairie dogs must always watch for danger.

A golden eagle can spot a prairie dog from over a mile away. It has amazing eyes!

DIVE DOWN

Rumble! The ground shakes. A prairie dog sprints back to it's burrow.

Prairie dogs hide from danger underground. Their burrows have many entrances. They can vanish in a flash!

Above ground, they run in zigzag paths. This makes them hard to catch. They stay near burrow holes when they eat.

They dig listening rooms near the entrance. These rooms help them hear predators coming.

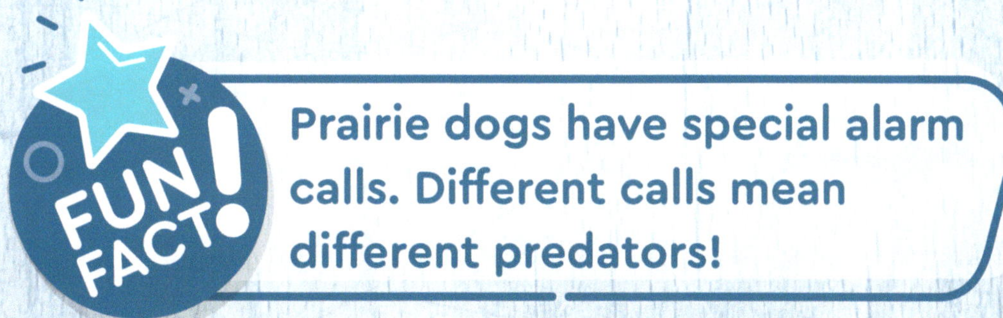

Prairie dogs have special alarm calls. Different calls mean different predators!

23

SCURRY FAST

All clear! A prairie dog runs out of his burrow to eat.

Prairie dogs run fast on four short legs. They can reach speeds of 35 miles per hour. That is faster than when you ride your bike!

They scurry low to the ground. Their bodies stay close to the dirt. This helps them move quickly.

When danger comes, they race to their burrows. A prairie dog is never far from a burrow entrance so it can dive underground in seconds

Prairie dogs cut down all the tall grass around their burrows. This gives them a clear view of danger and a straight path to run home!

BUSY DAYS

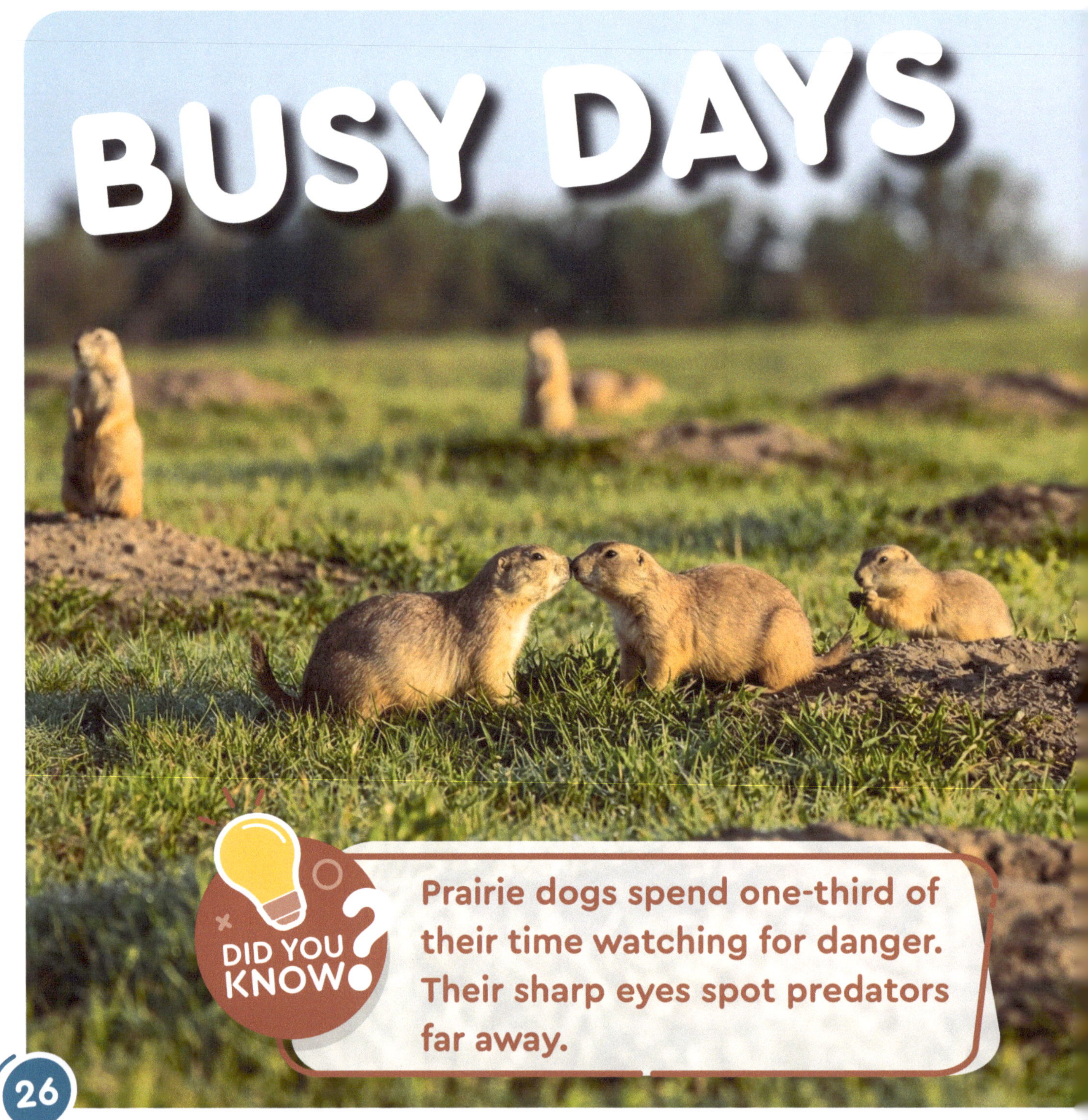

Prairie dogs spend one-third of their time watching for danger. Their sharp eyes spot predators far away.

Buzz! The prairie dog colony starts another busy day.

Prairie dogs are **diurnal**. This means they are active during the day. At night, they sleep in underground rooms.

Mornings are busy times. Prairie dogs come out to eat and groom. They spend hours nibbling grass near their burrows.

Afternoons can get hot. Some prairie dogs rest in cool tunnels. They come back out when it cools down. By sunset, they head underground to sleep.

TOWN TALK

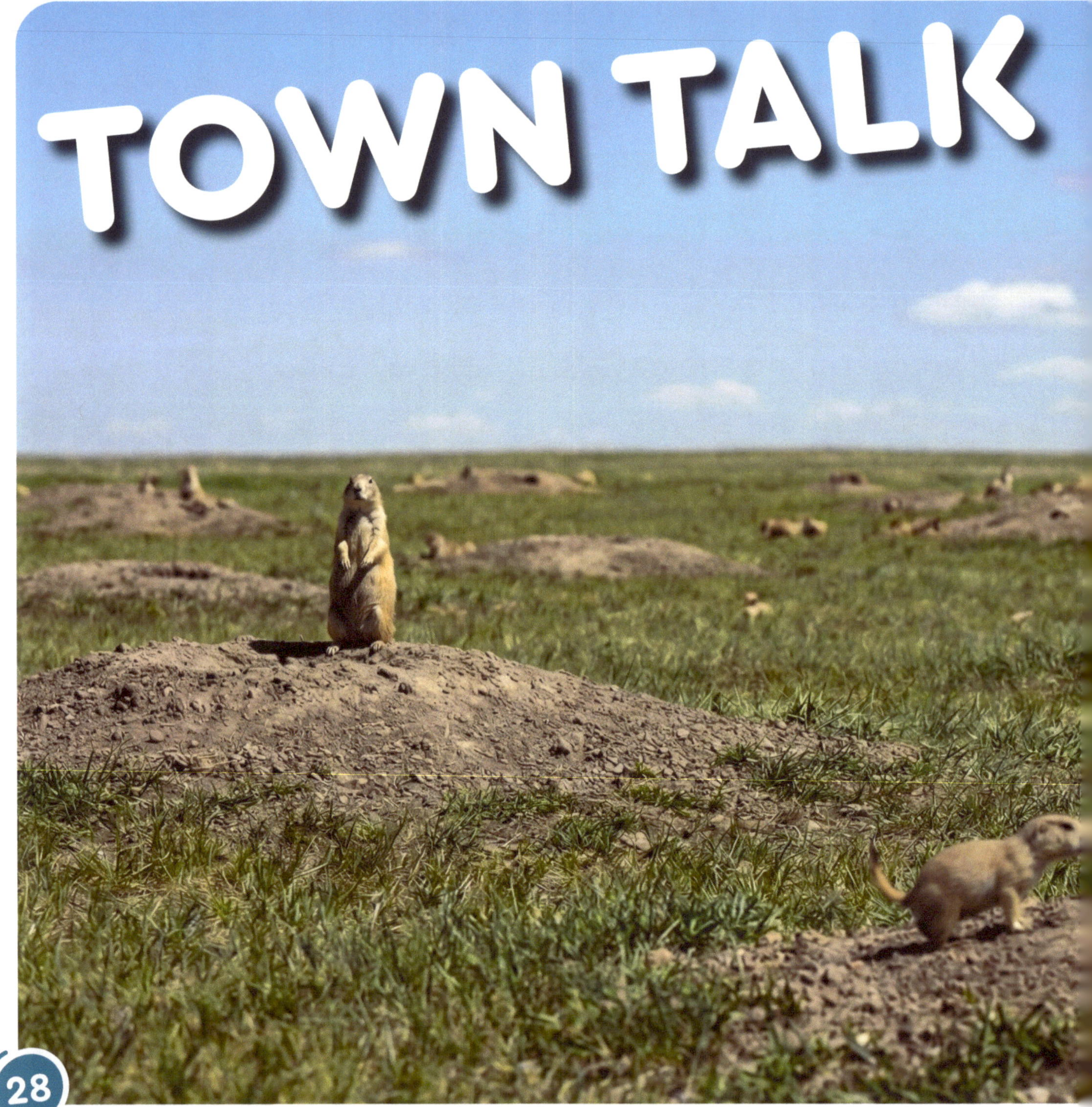

Chirp chirp! Prairie dogs chat in their busy town.

Prairie dogs live in big groups. These groups are called towns. A town can have hundreds of prairie dogs!

Towns have smaller family groups. These are called **coteries**. A coterie has one adult male. It has a few females too. It also has their babies. They share their homes. They share food areas too.

Families work as a team. They clean each other. They take turns watching for danger.

The biggest prairie dog town ever found had about 400 million prairie dogs in it!

29

PAIRING UP

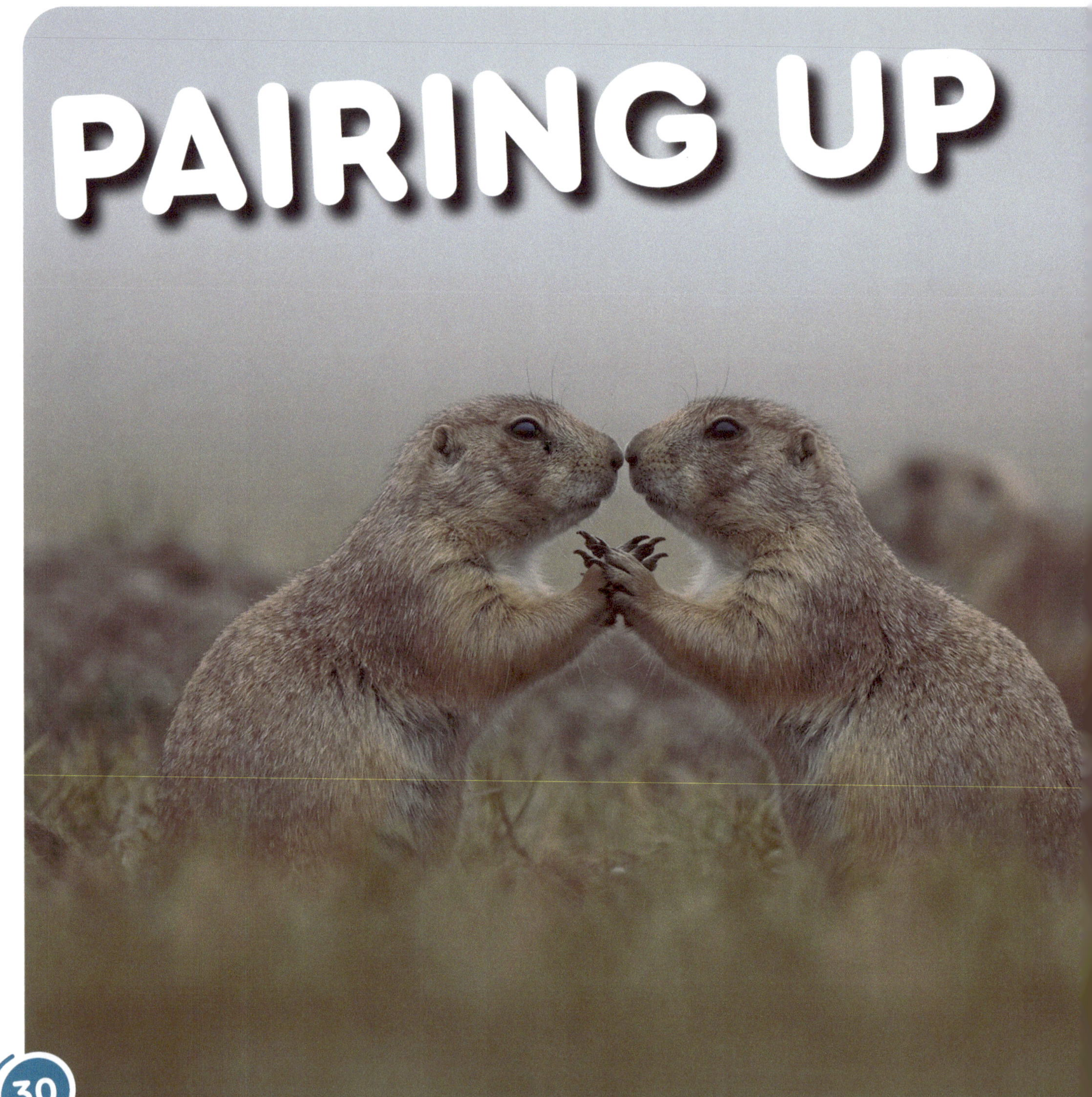

Touch! Two prairie dogs touch noses, they will be mates.

Prairie dogs mate in late winter. Most mate in February and March. The ground is still cold. But these busy animals are ready to find mates.

Males visit females in their coterie. They make soft clicking sounds. They wag their tails.

Females can only mate for one day each year. After mating, they go underground. They build a cozy nest for their babies.

Male prairie dogs lose weight during mating season. They spend so much time looking for mates that they forget to eat!

PRECIOUS PUPS

Climb! A young pup peeks up out of his burrow. Mom is close behind.

Baby prairie dogs are called pups. Mothers give birth underground in spring. Most litters have three to five pups.

Newborn pups are very tiny. They weigh less than one ounce! That is lighter than a slice of bread. Pups are born with no fur.

Pups cannot see or hear at first. They are born with their eyes and ears closed. Their eyes stay closed for about five weeks. This makes newborns completely helpless.

FAMILY FIRST

34

Sniff! A mother prairie dog gives the "all clear". Her pups can come out the explore.

Mother prairie dogs provide most of the care for their pups. They nurse them for about six weeks. Fathers help too by protecting the family and the burrow.

Pups first come outside at six weeks old. They are curious but stay close to mom. Pups learn what plants to eat by watching adults.

Other females in the coterie help watch the pups. Young males stay with their family for about one year, but females often stay for life.

TUNNEL TALENT

Break Time! A prairie dog takes a break from digging his tunnel.

Prairie dog tunnels can go up to 15 feet deep underground. That is deeper than most swimming pools! Some burrow systems stretch over 100 feet long.

Prairie dogs dig special rooms underground. They make bedrooms, bathrooms, and listening posts. Each room has its own job.

All this digging helps the land. The tunnels bring air and water into the soil.

Prairie dogs can move 400 pounds of dirt when building one burrow!

WHERE TO WATCH

Look! A prairie dog wakes up and stretches at dawn. You can spot one!

Want to see a prairie dog in the wild? Visit an open grassland in the early morning.

Look for flat areas covered in short grass with small dirt mounds.

Stay still and be very quiet. Prairie dogs are always watching for danger. If you move too fast, they will bark a warning and disappear underground in seconds.

Bring binoculars! Prairie dogs can spot you from far away, but with binoculars you can watch all their funny behavior without scaring them off.

GLOSSARY

colony
A big group of animals that live together in one place.

burrow
A hole or tunnel that an animal digs in the ground to live in.

predators
Animals that hunt and eat other animals.

diurnal
Active during the day and sleeping at night.

coteries
Small family groups of prairie dogs that live and work together.

9 7 9 8 8 9 8 1 8 1 6 9 7